The EZ Guide to Landscape Lighting

By

Bob Long

Table of Contents

Chapter 1

All About Landscape Lighting

In the U.S., families and individuals spend around $50 billion annually installing and maintaining landscaping for their homes. Homeowners are willing to invest this massive amount of money on improving the exterior of their residences because a beautiful yard is a source of satisfaction, a refuge from the stresses of everyday life and an outdoor extension of the home that can be enjoyed with family and friends.

Exterior lighting is a growing component of landscape design and a must for homeowners who want their property looking great day and night. The primary reasons for installing landscape lighting are:

- Strategically placed accent lights can bring out details in a house that otherwise would not be visible after dark. Landscape lighting can also be used to accent large bushes, trees, walkways and water features such as ponds, pools, waterfalls, and fountains. These highlights bring the night to life and give the property a serene, ethereal feeling.
- Landscape lighting increases the time that can be spent outdoors. Well lit patios, decks, pools, play areas and gardens can all be used for fun or to just relax day and night.
- Exterior lighting enhances safety and security. Hazards such as dark steps, abrupt changes in elevation, low hanging vegetation and obstructions on walkways can all be avoided when properly illuminated. Crime statistics also prove that a well-lit landscape deters potential intruders.
- Finally, landscape lighting not only increases the resident's enjoyment of their property, it usually enhances value, when it is time to sell.

Different Types of Landscape Lights are Available to Meet your Needs

When planning and installing landscape lighting there are a mind-numbing variety of alternatives that can be found in the marketplace. These include the power source, the type and size of bulbs and the appearance and material of the lighting fixtures. The number of possible alternatives is magnified because each of these basic components can be mixed and matched with the others. In other words, each of the power sources can use different types of light bulbs and each of light bulb types can be held in a large variety of fixtures. The light bulbs and fixtures in turn can project the light with different intensities, beams and colors. This book will cover these alternatives to help you find and install the lighting system that best meets your needs. Here is an overview of the topics that will be covered.

Power Supply

Exterior residential and business lighting systems are **powered** in 3 different ways.

- **Line or high-voltage** lighting refers to fixtures that are driven directly by the 120 volt electrical power that is standard in buildings in the US.

- o **Low-voltage systems** use a transformer that reduces the high-voltage output down to 12 volts.
- o **Solar-powered lighting** uses a solar cells or panel to convert energy from the sun into electricity. This energy is stored in batteries which are discharged after dark to power the light.

Light Bulbs

There are a **wide variety of light bulbs** that can be used for landscape lighting.

- o **Incandescent lights** are the traditional bulbs developed by Thomas Edison over 130 years ago. The incandescent bulb contains a filament, which glows and emits light when electricity flows through the filament.
- o **Compact fluorescent lights (CFL)** are gas-discharge lamps that use electricity to agitate mercury vapor. The excited mercury atoms produce short-wave ultraviolet light that then cause a phosphor to fluoresce, producing visible light.
- o **High-intensity discharge lamps (HID)** are a bulb that produces light by means of an electric arc between electrodes housed inside a gas filled tube. The primary tyes of HID lights used in outdoor lighting are metal halide, mercury vapor and high pressure sodium lamps.
- o **Halogen lamps** are high pressure incandescent lamps containing halogen gases such as iodine or bromine which allow the filaments to be operated at higher temperatures and higher efficacies. A high-temperature chemical reaction, involving tungsten and the halogen gas, recycles evaporated particles of tungsten back onto the filament surface extending the working life of the bulb.
- o **LED** stands for light emitting diode and is a solid-state semiconductor that converts electrical energy directly into light. On its most basic level, the semiconductor is comprised of two regions. The p-region contains positive electrical charges while the n-region contains negative electrical charges. When voltage is applied and current begins to flow, the electrons move across the n region into the p region. This process of an electron moving through the p-n junction releases energy which is dispersed in the form of light.

In addition to the size and brightness, light bulbs are also distinguished by the **beam or spread of the light** as it is projected outward. This breadth and direction of the beam is a function of both the focus of the lamp and the fixture into which it is fitted. Here are some examples:

- **Spot-lights** are accent lights that generally highlight building features, plants or significant fixtures on the property. The beam in a spot light is tightly focused
- **Flood lights** are similar to spotlights but the angle at which the light is projected is much wider and hence flood lights are used to illuminate broad spaces like play areas or basketball courts rather than highlighting a single feature.
- **Path Lights** are downward projecting lights that illuminate paths and walkways spreading beams over the ground.
- **Bollards** are Omni directional lights that sit on top of a post or pole. These lights are also commonly known as beacon lights.
- **Aquatic lights** are used to highlight water features such as a pool, pond, waterfall or fountain

Before getting into the details of designing landscape lighting systems, in the next chapter, we present a glossary of common lighting terms. This book is full of useful information to help the DIY homeowner including:

Chapter 2

Lighting Terminology

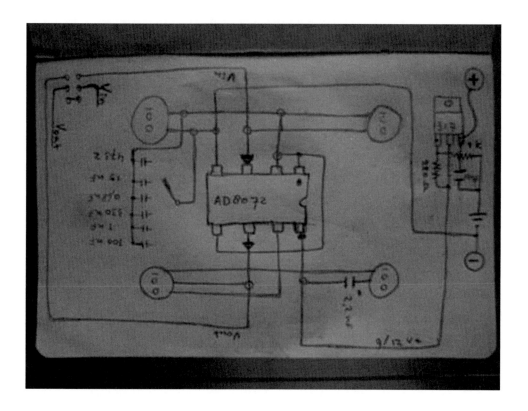

Here are some common lighting terms that we will use in this book in describing how to make your property standout after dark.

Amps: A measure of electrical current or the amount of charge passing a point in an electric circuit per unit time. Think of it as analogous to the flow rate of water in a pipe, in other words, the volume of water that passes by a point in the pipe over a set period of time i.e. gallons per minute.

Ballast: A device used with all fluorescent and HID lights to obtain the necessary circuit conditions for starting and operating the lamp.

Daisy Chain: Running lights in a series on a single cable. Too many lights in a long chain lead to a drop in voltage and lights with inconsistent intensity.

For a consistent illumination avoid putting more than 3 or 4 lights in a daisy chain on a single able run.

Efficacy: The efficacy of a light bulb is a measure of the amount of light given off for the amount of electrical energy input. The common metric is lumens per kilowatt-hour.

Energy: A measure of work done by an electrical system over a given period of time, often expressed in kilowatt-hours (KWH). A kilowatt-hour is 1000 watts consumed over 1 hour and is the unit of energy that is the basis for your electrical bill.

Footcandle: A measure of luminance or light falling onto a surface. One footcandle is the light given off by a candle at a distance of one foot and is equal to 1 lumen per square foot.

Junction Box: Also known as a hub this device is an alternative to daisy chains. The junction box is connected to the power supply by a single cable and evenly distributes electrical power to the multiple light fixtures that are in turn connected to the box

Low-Voltage Lighting System: A type of lighting that operates on 12-volt current rather than the standard 120 volts. Power is supplied by a transformer, which is plugged into a standard 120-volt electrical outlet.

Lumens: The amount of light that a bulb produces on a given area of surface. One lumen per square foot equals 1 footcandle which is the brightness of a candle seen at a distance of 1 foot. A standard 100-watt incandescent bulb typically produces about 1600 lumens.

Lumen Efficacy: Efficiency of a light source expressed in lumens per watt (LPW or lm/W). Lumens measure the intensity of light given off by the bulb and watts represent the consumption of electrical power. So LPW is an indicator of the cost of providing a unit of illumination. Landscape lights that output more illumination (lumens), while consuming less energy (watts) result in lower electric bills. So LPW is an indicator of the cost of providing a unit of illumination.

Photovoltaic (PV): This is the fancy name for a solar cell that converts sunlight directly into electricity. Solar cells are often used to power calculators and watches and are made of semiconducting materials similar to those used in computer chips. When sunlight is absorbed by these materials, the solar energy knocks electrons loose from their atoms, allowing the electrons to flow through the material to produce electricity. This process of converting light (photons) to electricity (voltage) is called the photovoltaic effect.

Rated Life (RTL): The median expected life of light bulbs that is based on lab tests of a large sample of representative lamps. The "average life" is the point in hours when 50% of the bulbs are still operating.

Spectrum: Spectrum refers to the different color temperatures on the Kelvin scale of illumination given off by various sources of light. For example, warmer (lower color temperature) light is a long time characteristic of incandescent bulbs and is most often used in the home or public areas to promote relaxation. These warmer colors appear yellowish white to red to the human eye. Cooler colors (higher color temperature) as found in fluorescent lights appear bluish, white and are commonly used to enhance concentration in offices. Please note that for whatever strange reasons, warmer colors have a lower color temperature on the Kelvin scale and cooler colors have a higher temperature. Confusing, maybe, but not a typo.

Transformer: Also known as the power supply, the transformer converts 120 volt electricity to 12 volts resulting in a much safer electrical supply.

Voltage: Measurement for the electromotive force, or the pressure of electricity. Household voltage in the United States, nominally 120 volts, varies between 110 and 125 volts.

Voltage Drop: Voltage decreases as electricity travels along low-voltage cable. The amount of voltage drop depends on the gauge of the wire, length of the cable run, and the total number of watts consumed by lights connected to the cable. As voltage drops, light output decreases and when there is excessive voltage drop, fixtures at the end of the cable will produce noticeably less light and color of light than fixtures closer to the transformer.

Watt: A unit of electrical power. Lamps are rated in watts to indicate their power consumption and intensity of light. Power consumed over time equals the electrical energy used. Generally electric bills are charged to consumers at rate per kilowatt hour. A kilowatt hour is 1000 watts of electrical power consumed for 1 hour.

Watts vs. Voltage vs. Amps: The best way to understand the differences between these three metrics is to use the analogy of water flowing through a hose. Voltage is then the equivalent of water pressure, current, which is measured in amps, is the flow rate of the water through the hose and watts is the force of the water as it comes out of the hose. In an electrical system, power equals voltage multiplied by amps. The analogy holds since you can increase the force of the water coming out of the hose by increasing either the water pressure or the flow rate.

Chapter 3

Understanding Low-Voltage Lighting

Low-Voltage vs. Line-Voltage

Line or high-voltage lighting refers to fixtures that are powered directly by the 120 volt electricity that is the standard output of power companies in the US. For existing light fixtures that are on or very close to the house, line-voltage lights can be replaced or upgraded by individuals who have at least a competent level of handyman skills. However setting up a new line-voltage circuit, especially when remote from the main dwelling, needs a skilled electrician and often also requires permits from the local government. Line-voltage cable must be buried 1.5 -2 feet deep depending on local codes and exposure to severe shock is always a risk.

In low-voltage lighting there's a transformer that reduces the high-voltage output down to 12 volts. Low-voltage lights have many advantages over high-voltage alternatives that make them a preferred alternative for outdoor landscaping projects, particularly DIY projects.

Advantages of Low-Voltage Systems

Low-voltage lighting is the most common option for outdoor landscaping projects for many reasons. It is less expensive to operate and safer than high-voltage systems particularly near wet locations. It does not require a licensed electrician to install and the power cable does not need to be in a conduit and buried. The connections from the cable to the light fixtures can be as simple as pressing pins into a wire. Additionally there are far more choices of low-voltage landscape lighting fixtures, bulbs and designs.

In low-voltage lighting the connecting wire can be buried a few inches underground or even just run on the surface in areas with little-to-no traffic. Because a low-voltage system only runs between 10-15 volts, it does not pose a safety hazard. This leads to a lot of flexibility in testing alternative layouts or making future modifications. Most individuals are quite capable of installing and maintaining low-voltage outdoor lighting on their own. So while professional lighting installers can save time and may do superior work, many "Do It Yourselfers" can safely install beautiful and functional low-voltage lighting designs and avoid the expense of paying someone to do the work.

Outdoor low-voltage systems offer a great selection of fixtures and lights that are generally smaller and easier to blend into the terrain than components that typically come with line-voltage systems. Low-voltage light bulbs come in a variety of technologies including halogen, incandescent, compact fluorescent, HID and LED lamps. Halogen lights are the most common type of bulb used in low-voltage systems today, but all the above are alternatives worth considering. Each of these types of bulbs has different initial purchase costs, life expectancy and efficacy. We will evaluate these pluses and minuses in much more detail in Chapter 6 of this book.

A common misunderstanding is that low-voltage lights automatically consume less electricity because they are a "low-voltage." But electricity usage is driven by the total wattage of the light bulbs in the system, not the underlying voltage. So a 200 watt, 120 volt system will use the same power as an equivalent 200 watt, low-voltage system. It may even use more because the transformer itself consumes some power. However, most low-voltage light bulbs have much higher efficacy and output 2X to 3X more lumens for the same wattage as standard incandescent bulbs. So you can easily design a low-voltage system that gives off the same amount of light as a line-voltage system but consumes only ½ to ⅓ the electricity by following the guidelines in this book. The potential annual savings on your electrical bill is significant and can be estimated using the following formula:

(Line System Total Watts – Low-Voltage Watts) x average hours operated per day x days per year operated x cost per kilowatt hour /1000.

The cost per kilowatt hour varies by location with a range roughly from 7 cents per KWH in North Dakota to 26 cents in Hawaii. These numbers are subject to change at any time and are only intended to illustrate the typical range in costs by geography. The rate in your location can be found on your electric bill and should include taxes and any other regulatory fees.

Here is a sample calculation based on an example of replacing ten 100 watt incandescent lights with ten 50 watt halogen lights that produce at least the same amount of illumination. For this example, we will assume an average electrical cost of 15 cents per kilowatt hour.

> High-Voltage System = 1,000 total watts
> Low-Voltage System = 500 watts
> Average Operating Hours per day = 10 hours
> Days operated per year = 365
> Savings = (1000-500) x 10 x 365 x .15 /1000 = $274 per year.

For systems with more lights, higher utilization or in locations with higher power costs this annual savings will become much greater.

Chapter 4

Design Low-Voltage Lighting Like a Pro

10 Steps to Design and Install Low Voltage Lighting

Here is a 10 step DIY process for designing and installing a low-voltage landscape lighting system:

1. **Locate a covered outdoor GFCI AC outlet**(s) to power your system. Plan on mounting the transformer(s) within 1 foot of the outlet(s). It is

best not to use an extension cord for this connection. Depending on the size and distance you are covering, you may need multiple outlets and transformers. If you cannot use a convenient GFCI outlet on the outside of your home, you will need a certified electrician to install one.

2. **Estimate the number, location and total wattage of the lights you plan to install.** The capacity and design of the all other components of the lighting system are driven by this estimate. We will use the plan shown below in figure 1 to illustrate how this works:

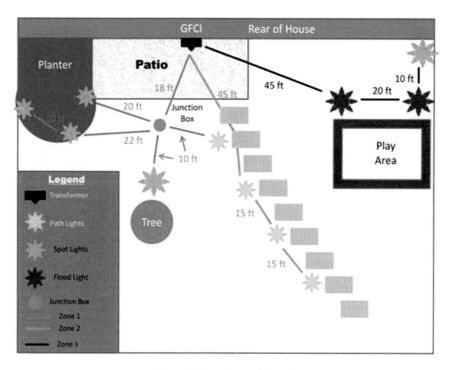

Figure 1: Landscape Layout

This lighting system has eleven lights total that we divided into 3 zones based on proximity to the transformer.

- One 35 watt spot light highlighting a section of the rear of the house
- One 50 watt spot light highlighting a tree in the yard
- Three 20 watt spot lights highlighting plants in the planter
- Four 20 watt path lights
- Two 50 watt flood lights illuminating the play area

- Three zones, 2 daisy chains and one junction box

3. **Determine the required capacity for the power supply.** Power supplies or transformers are rated by the wattage they output. The basic guideline is that the watts consumed by all the connected lights and devices cannot exceed the rating of the transformer. In actual practice, we try not to exceed 75% - 80% of the transformers output to allow for future changes. The planned design in figure 1 calls for three 50 watt bulbs, seven 20 watt bulbs, and one 35 watt bulb for a total of 325 watts. Applying the allowance increases this to around 400 watts. This capacity can be met by one relatively large transformer or multiple smaller ones. In this example we will opt for a single 400 watt power supply.

4. **Design the cable runs so that the drop in voltage never exceeds 10% or 1.2 volts for a 12 volt system.** One of the keys to installing professional-looking landscape lighting is the consistent intensity of the illumination output by the individual bulbs regardless of their distance from the transformer. Several methods can be used individually or in combination to achieve this result. These include segmenting the lighting fixtures into zones with separate cable runs, decreasing the gauge of the cable, using splices and junction boxes to minimize daisy chains and varying the output of voltage at the source with a multi tap transformer.

5. In our example in figure 1, we **group the light fixtures into zones that are defined to minimize the differences in distance from the transformer.** By having 3 zones, the length of any cable run with daisy chained light fixtures is much less that it would be in a design with only one zone. The shorter the cable run, the smaller the voltage drop.

6. Since we opted for a single power supply and multiple zones, **the transformer should have a sufficient number of output terminals to connect cables from each zone.** Multi tap transformers as shown in figure 2. can vary the voltage output from the terminals typically ranging

between 12 and 15 volts. The higher voltage terminals can be used to compensate voltage drop for bigger zones.

Figure 2: Multi Tap Transformer

7. The *lower* the gauge of the cable the *thicker* the wire is. Thicker wire can carry more voltage and mitigate any potential loss over the run. But lower gauge cable is also more expensive so for smaller cable runs when voltage drop is not an issue, you can use a higher gauge.

8. Knowing the wattage, the length of the cable run in each zone and gauge of the wire, we can calculate voltage drop as follows:

Voltage Drop = [Total Watts in the zone x Cable Length]/Cable Constant

The cable constant depends on the gauge of wire that is used to connect the lights and the power supply as is shown below in Table 1:

Cable Gauge	Cable Constant
16	2200
14	3500
12	7500
10	11920

Table 1: Cable Constants for Calculating Voltage Drop

We start with the assumption of standard 12 gauge cable and estimate the voltage drop for each zone in our plan using a constant of 7500.

In Zone 1, we use a junction box which mitigates the impact of voltage drop so the only potential issue is with the daisy chain in the planter.

The voltage drop in this segment of the zone is calculated as (18 ft + 22 ft + 10 ft) x 2 x 20 watts /7500 = 0.27 volts and is well within the 10% guideline for loss.

In Zone 2, voltage drop = (45 ft + 15 ft +15 ft) x (3 x 20) watts /7500 = 0.60 volts and once again is within 10%

In Zone 3, (45 ft + 20 ft + 10 ft) x (3 x 50) watts/7500 =1.5 volts and exceeds the 10% limit.

To mitigate this loss, we can use 10-gauge cable. This would change the voltage drop calculation to (45 ft + 20 ft + 10 ft) x (3 x 50) watts/11920 = .94 volts which is within the 10% limit. Another alternative would be to divide the run into two zones.

Both alternatives accomplish the objective of bringing the voltage drop back within 10% or 1.2 volts.

9. Other features that we prefer in a transformer are a photoelectric cell to turn the unit on and a timer to turn it off. We use the photoelectric cell as the "On" switch since it adjusts automatically to seasonal changes in the onset of darkness. We prefer using a timer as the "Off" switch since we can set a length of time for the lights to stay on as opposed to waiting for daybreak. So we recommend selecting a transformer that either has these

features built in or adding them as a separate component to the power hook up.

10. After all the lighting fixtures are in place and connected to the transformer, test the system after dark to see if it achieves the desired effect. Once you are happy with the results, bury the cable a couple of inches underground in the open areas or cover with mulch or weed blocker in the planter areas. It is absolutely necessary to bury the cable? No, exposed cable is weatherproof and shock less. However, for esthetics and to avoid the cable being damaged by children, pets, lawnmowers etc, or causing accidents it is a good idea to go the extra mile and make sure that the cable is safely tucked away under turf, mulch, rocks or weed block fabric.

Chapter 5

Understanding Solar Powered Landscape Lighting

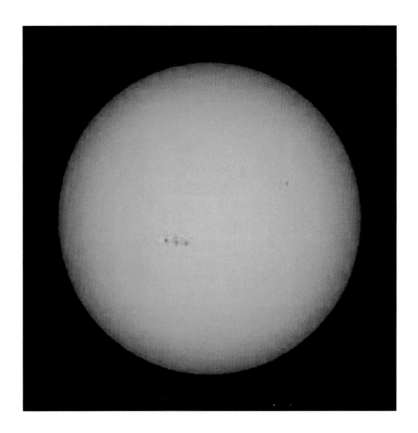

How do Solar Lights Work?

Outdoor solar lights use photovoltaic (PV) cells or panels to convert sunlight into electricity. The electricity is stored in batteries or capacitors and then released for use by the lamp at night. Photoelectric sensors activate the lights at sunset and turn them off at sunrise. In recent years advances made in PV cells, rechargeable batteries and capacitors have made this technology much more practical and dependable. Most solar landscape lights will run for about eight to ten hours per night if they receive a full charge during the day. They will function in cold weather locations but since the availability of sunlight during winter months is less, expect the "on" time to also be reduced. Despite these improvements, quality low-voltage systems can still put out more light than equivalent solar lights and can operate all night with equal luminosity while solar lights start losing their strength within several hours.

Advantages of Solar Lighting

The main advantage of solar lighting is that the light fixtures can be placed almost anywhere in your yard without running cable. You can add as many fixtures as you like without the constraints of power supply capacity or needing to add zones to maintain voltage over long cable runs. The only restriction is that the PV panels that power the lights must have access to sunlight. For lights with a built in PV cell, this eliminates placing the lamp in shady areas. However many powered lights have detachable PV cells that can be located some distance from the light fixture. These lights can be located anywhere as long the cell itself is exposed directly to the sunlight. The downside is that this may re-create the need to bury the connecting wire.

Installation is generally as easy as pushing a small post into the ground and the lighting can be used in locations at any distance from the house since there is no need for GFCI access. The energy cost, other than battery replacement from time to time, is zero. There is no need for a transformer or balancing voltage across the system.

Solar lighting is a good option under the following conditions:

- o There is no problem with sunlight during any part of the year in the locations where you need the light.
- o The location where you want lighting does not have access to an electrical supply
- o You don't mind somewhat less illumination per fixture or that the lights will not always stay on through the entire night
- o Or you are like us and just think that collecting energy from the sun is cool.

Solar Lighting Guidelines

 If you opt to go with solar powered landscape lighting here are some guidelines to follow:

- o Solar landscape lighting comes in a variety of styles from various manufacturers. We prefer fixtures that are made of die-cast metal for durability and styling detail.
- o If you place the lights in the shade of a large tree or under a bush make sure you use lights that have a detachable PV so you can maximize the sunlight received during the day.
- o Only buy models that are designed to be completely weather and waterproof.
- o Do not place lights in locations where ambient light from other sources such as street lamps can cause the photoelectric cell to erroneously turn the light off
- o Buy lights with "amorphous" solar panels which can pick up power even on cloudy days and do not require direct sunlight.
- o Buy lights that use NiCad (Nickel Cadmium) rechargeable batteries. Make sure the rechargeable batteries that come with your lights are replaceable. Many of these batteries come in the AA size and are readily available at most hardware stores.
- o Use LED bulbs to maximize efficiency and extend "on" times.

The Future of Solar Landscape Lighting

In the past, solar lights were (and many still are) weak and cannot hold a consistent charge for more than a few hours. More recently, solar lighting designers and engineers have been able to use advanced light emitting diode lamps that draw minimal current yet provide intense light output. These lights are more expensive but they draw much less power which extends the "on" time for a given charge. LED lamps are so efficient that one lamp can last for years before being replaced. We will discuss the pluses and minuses of the different types of light bulbs that are used in landscape lighting in Chapter 6.

Currently most solar lights are powered by rechargeable batteries. To recharge these batteries requires extended exposure to sunlight and after dark; the power output begins to decline after only several hours of operation. Due to their use of chemical reactions, most rechargeable batteries can only last for one year before needing to be replaced.

Ultracapacitors are a newly developed technology positioned between conventional capacitors and rechargeable batteries that avoid the typical battery problems of limited cycle life, degraded performance during cold weather and slow charging rates. Although the total energy output of an ultracapacitor is less than what can be obtained through rechargeable batteries, it is sufficient to power solar lights. Because ultracapacitors transfer electrical charges between conducting materials, they can be charged and discharged almost indefinitely eliminating batteries' need for replacement. In addition, the ultracapacitor can also be charged effectively. regardless of the prevailing weather conditions. Manufacturers are claiming recharge times of 3 hours in full sun and 8 hours when cloudy or raining.

So in theory, solar lighting with a metal fixture, LED bulb and ultracapacitor should provide a long-lasting and dependable form of landscape lighting that is very easy to install and requires virtually no maintenance. Occasionally you may have to wipe down the solar panel but that is it. But recognize that LEDs powered by ultracapacitors are a new technology that is still only available from a handful of vendors. We have not had any hands on experience using solar lights with ultracapacitors and are only reiterating information on this subject that was found on the internet. However, we do think that in time this technology has the capability to advance solar lighting to be the preferred solution for residential landscape lighting.

Before purchasing any solar lights, we suggest buying one fixture of the brand, type and model that you are interested in and testing it in the different locations you plan to illuminate to determine how it actually works. Since solar lighting is so easy to install and move around this is a worthwhile investment of your time to ensure that you are satisfied with the performance. We have found that solar lights, especially the less expensive ones, do not necessarily live up to the hype presented by manufacturers and vendors.

Chapter 6

Landscape Light Bulbs

Types of Landscape Light Bulbs

We categorize outdoor light bulbs into 5 major categories; incandescent, tungsten halogen, fluorescent, high intensity discharge (HID) and light emitting diodes (LED).

Incandescent Bulbs

Incandescent bulbs produce light when an electric current passes through a filament and causes it to glow. These are the type of bulbs that most people think of when the word "light bulb" is mentioned. They are used extensively inside homes and in outside landscaping in fixtures that are connected to line-voltage source from the house. They give off a warm yellow white light that most people prefer and are very inexpensive. However, they not very efficient (low efficacy) and waste much of their energy through heat loss. They are best used for lighting tasks that demand high levels of brightness. The unfortunate U.S. Energy and Independence Act of 2007, requires most incandescent bulbs to produce the same amount of light while using less wattage. This is having the effect of forcing these popular, low cost bulbs off the market with the intent of replacing them with compact fluorescent bulbs.

Fluorescent

Fluorescent bulbs produce light when an electric arc passes between cathodes to excite mercury and other gases producing radiant energy, which is then converted to visible light by a phosphor coating. They use 1/5 to 1/3 as much electricity as incandescent bulbs with comparable lumen ratings and last up to 20 times longer. Fluorescent bulbs are also very efficient, producing very little heat. In general, they are ideal for lighting large areas where little detail work needs to be done.

A common misconception is that all fluorescent lamps are neutral or cool in color appearance and do not have very good color-rendering ability. This is largely due to the fact that historically "cool white" fluorescent tube lamps were the industry standard. For example, I always thought my skin looked green under these old fluorescent lights. This is no longer the case and modern fluorescent lamps offer much better color rendition and a range of color temperature choices. Compact screw-in types (CFL) can be used in place of incandescent light bulbs in standard lamp sockets and are available in a wide spectrum of colors. Warm white tones best duplicate the color of incandescent bulbs. All fluorescent bulbs need components called ballasts to provide the right amount of voltage.

Two complaints about CFLs' are that they are more expensive to purchase and take some time after the switch is thrown to fully light the room. Newer technology quick start CFL's have largely addressed the delay problem for most people. Because fluorescent bulbs contain mercury, it is also important to dispose of them properly. Outside fluorescent bulbs are typically used as alternatives to incandescent bulbs in posts lamps, pendants, flood lights and wall lights.

Figure 3: Fluorescent Flood Light

Tungsten-halogen

Tungsten-halogen bulbs are a variation of the incandescent light that works by passing electricity through a tungsten filament, which is enclosed in a tube containing halogen gas. The halogen gas causes a chemical reaction to take place, removing tungsten from the wall of the glass and depositing it back onto the filament, thereby extending the life of the bulb. Halogen lamps produce a brilliant white light and are more efficient (more lumens per watt) than standard incandescent bulbs. They are also more expensive than standard light bulbs. Halogen bulbs are available in both line-voltage (120 watt) and low-voltage (12 volt) styles. The line-voltage version is generally used as a longer lasting, more efficient version of the regular incandescent light. Low-voltage halogen lights are the standard bulbs that come with many landscape lighting kits. Models MR8, MR11 and MR16 (mini-reflectors) provide excellent beam control, and are popularly used in landscaping to highlight outdoor features at night. Their small size enables them to be more easily blended into the terrain than the generally larger 120 volt fixtures.

Figure 4: Halogen Light Bulbs

High intensity Discharge Bulbs (HID)

HID bulbs produce light when an arc passes between cathodes in a pressurized tube, causing metallic additives to vaporize. They have long lives and are extremely energy efficient, but generally do not produce pleasing light colors. There are two basic types of HIDs that are used in residential lighting, Metal Halide and High-Pressure Sodium. Compared to fluorescent and incandescent bulbs, HID lamps produce a large quantity of light from a relatively small bulb. Standard high-pressure sodium lamps have a higher efficacy then Metal Halide, but they produce a yellowish light. Metal halide lamps are less efficient but produce a whiter, more natural color. HID lamps are typically used not only when energy efficiency and/or long-life are desired, but also when high levels of light are required to be projected over large areas. In residential landscaping, HIDs are often used for outdoor security and area lighting.

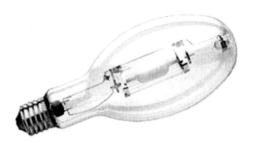

Figure 5: HID Bulb

Light Emitting Diodes (LED)

LEDs produce light when voltage is applied to negatively charged semiconductors, causing electrons to combine and create a unit of light (photon). In simpler terms, an LED is a chemical chip embedded in a plastic capsule. Because they are small, several LEDs are sometimes combined to produce a single light bulb. LED lighting in general is more efficient and longer lasting than any other type of light source, and it is being developed for more and more residential applications. In particular use of LEDs for outdoor landscape is becoming increasingly popular. LED lighting is 80 percent more efficient than traditional incandescent bulbs and over 10% more efficient than CFL's. LEDs are ultra compact, produce minimal heat and do not contain any mercury or other toxic material which simplifies disposal. Of course, you will rarely ever have to dispose of them. With a 50,000 hour RTL, if you install an LED in a newborn baby's room and operate it 8 hour per day every day, it is likely that you won't have to change-out the bulb until after that infant is off to college.

I believe LED's are the future of lighting and will soon supplant CFLs, halogen and incandescent bulbs both inside the home and outdoors. Chapter 10 discusses the development of LEDs in more detail.

Figure 6: LED Light

Chapter 7

Landscape Lighting Fixtures

Types of Landscape Lights

Landscape lights are used for many different purposes. In this chapter, we will cover spot lights, flood lights, path lights, bollards and security lights. A special category of underwater lights is covered separately in Chapter 9. Each of these categories is defined by the characteristics of the bulb and the shape of the lighting fixture that holds it.

Spot-Lights

Spotlights use bulbs that provide a bright light source with optics that output a focused beam. They are usually placed in fixtures that project light in a single direction. In landscaping, spotlights are most often used as accent lights that highlight and shadow houses, walls, trees, large plants or other prominent objects on a property. They are typically staked in the ground and project light upwards but they are also sometimes placed in trees, shining downwards to simulate moonlight. To add variety and enhance the natural colors in plants, red, yellow or blue filters are sometimes used with spotlights. Low-voltage spot lights generally use MR 16 bulbs between 20 to 50 watts.

Figure 7: Spot Light

Flood Lights

Flood lights work much the same as spotlights, but cast a less focused, wider beam. They are placed in fixtures that also facilitate a broader spread of light. This makes them ideal for lighting across wide expanses, such as play or work areas. These lights typically are situated above entryways, garage doors, sheds and patios. Flood lights are also commonly used as outside security lighting. When used in conjunction with motion sensors that activate when a person or object crosses the area of detection, they can greatly enhance the safety and security of a property without consuming much electricity.

Path Lights

Path lighting keeps driveways, walkways and garden paths safe for walking at night. Path light fixtures come in a variety of materials and designs but usually are low to the ground and have a domed top that directs the light downward in a spread pattern. Path lights also typically come with a choice of ground stakes, flange mounts and hanging hooks, to provide a wide choice of positioning options. Path lighting is usually sold in sets and includes both low-voltage and solar designs. Outdoor path lights add functional and aesthetic value to any property and are an integral component of the overall landscape. Path lighting can make a yard appear bigger than it really is and otherwise dark and forbidding places on the property safe and accessible for family and guests. For best results, path lights are staggered to illuminate a meandering walkway through the garden creating a magical, ethereal effect that is perfect for a safe after dark stroll. The appeal of path lighting is also not limited to nighttime. During daylight hours, these fixtures are visual accessories to highlight your garden walkways. Outdoor path lighting comes in a wide array of materials, shapes, sizes and designs. Plastic light fixtures are the least expensive and effective when the budget for landscaping is limited. Copper, aluminum and stainless steel lights cost more but are much more durable and generally present a richer, more stylish appearance. Designs for path light fixtures range from antique to ultra modern. Relatively dim light bulbs from 10 to 20 watts are used for outside path lighting since excessive light can be overbearing and ruin the overall effect. It is important that path lights are positioned to illuminate the path, but also placed so that they avoid being kicked, moved, or getting in the way of the lawnmower

Figure 8: Path Light

Bollards

Bollards, also known as beacon lights, are a type of architectural outdoor lighting that is composed of a short, upright ground-mounted post usually 1 to 3 feet in height with a lamp on top that typically casts light in multiple directions. They are often used to light or section off walkways, steps, and roadways. They differ from traditional path lights in that they focus light horizontally instead of the beam being directed downward onto the walkway,

30

and the light bulbs used are generally much brighter. The term bollard was originally used to describe the type of post sailors used to tie their ships to the dock or pier. To this day many bollard light fixtures retain a bit of that nautical look. Commercially, bollards are used to section off open space, for instance to keep vehicles from entering a restricted pedestrian area, or to add protection between a road and a walkway. Lighted bollards or beacon lights have the added functionally of illuminating the area at night. These durable post lights can also be used to light specific areas such as signs, company logos or otherwise dark stairways. Residentially, these lights are used to provide definition, separation or protection along walkways or to outline an area of a yard such as a patio or terrace. In addition, bollards can be used to enhance security of a property. A row of these bright lights can illuminate an area of a home or business enough to ward off intruders. Historically used in commercial applications around businesses and offices, bollards are becoming more popular in residential settings. Since home-owners favor more decorative landscape lighting, beacon light fixtures are now available in more designs and colors than the traditional black post. Bollards have multiple uses whether you are looking for decorative or functional landscape lighting.

Figure 9: Bollard

Security Lights

Flood lights and motion detectors can quickly and easily be installed to increase home security. Outdoor lights with motion detection will turn on automatically when something or someone moves within the vicinity of the exterior of the home exposing any potential intruders. Security lights also

31

provide a sense of safety to owners who arrive at home when it's dark. The security lights will turn on as you approach the door allowing you to more easily see the key slot and enter safely. Motion-activated security lights can also save money since the lights are only on when there is movement instead consuming electricity all night long. These floodlights should be installed near each entry door, garage door, or any other access point around your home.

Figure 10: Twin Security Flood Lights

Underwater Lighting

Under water lighting that is designed for use with ponds, fountains, waterfall and other aquatic features is covered in Chapter 9.

Chapter 8

Landscape Lighting Ideas

Design Concepts and Lighting Effects

In developing a lighting plan, there are several design concepts and lighting effects that are applicable to both low-voltage and solar powered landscape lighting.

More is Less or is it Less is More?

Do not try to light the entire area like a night game at a ballpark. Not only is that expensive, but it creates a flat harsh appearance that is not at all attractive. Good lighting designs create soft, enchanting pools of light balanced across the landscape. So the separation between fixtures generally should exceed the adjacent light so there are alternating bright and dark areas.

Quality Counts: Metal Beats Plastic

Metal light fixtures are more expensive but they are more durable and in our opinion look much better. Don't forget that any lights you install will be visible during the daytime hours so appearance matters.

Locate Fixtures in Plant Beds When Possible

Whenever possible locate the light fixtures in plant beds rather than the open lawn. Outdoor lights are subject to enough damage and misdirection from animals, children and the elements. Do not also expose them to lawn mowers and edge trimmers when it can be avoided. If a light has to be on the open lawn, we try to surround it with rocks or other natural looking barriers so it has some protection.

Verify the spectrum of the bulbs before purchasing

In addition to size, wattage and lumens, light bulbs usually come in a variety of colors or spectrums. High Pressure Sodium lights give off a yellow glow. Standard CFL, Metal Halide and LEDs give off a "colder" white light, which some like, but many people find displeasing. But all three of these bulbs now come in warmer color versions. There is no right and wrong in selecting spectrum, it is just what light you are most comfortable in for the activities you are undertaking. Spectrum is measured by color temperature as shown in the bar in Figure 11. The extremes are light under a Blue Sky at 10,000 degrees Kelvin and Candle light at 1000 degrees. The standard Incandescent bulb that people are used to from their living room is around 2,700 degrees.

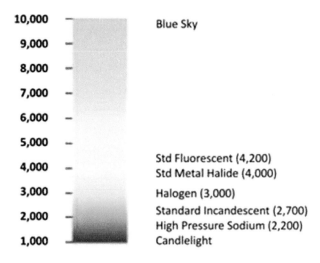

Figure 11: Color Spectrum

For the sake of simplicity we also divide it into four broader classes in the table below:

Classification	Degrees Kelvin	Description
Warm White	2,700 - 3,500	Standard incandescent bulbs that you find in peoples' living rooms
Natural White	3,500 - 4,500	Regular fluorescent Lighting that you find in a retail store
Daylight White	4,500 - 6,000	Noon day Sun
Cool White	6,000 - 7,000	Bright white light used in commercial facilities like hospitals

Table 1: Light Classifications

For most people, bulbs that fall in the Warm White and Natural White classes are preferred for landscape lighting.

Landscape Lighting Special Effects

You can use lighting techniques to highlight important features and create contrast in your yard and property. These include corners, angles and overhangs on the exterior of your home and trees, plants, statues, structures and water features.

Highlighting

This is perhaps the most common technique in outdoor lighting. Highlighting is formed by placing a spotlight at the base of a prominent section of the house or a tree or plant or a man-made structure in the yard and projecting light upwards. The corners of the house are common targets to be highlighted as well as recessed areas and turreted segments on the building. Trees, large plants or aquatic features such as waterfalls or fountains can also be brought to life after dark by highlighting with spotlights. By varying the distance, angle and number of the light fixtures, you can experiment with different lighting designs and effects.

Figure 12: Highlighting a Tree

Silhouetting

Silhouette lighting is a less commonly used lighting effect that enables the designer to accomplish two things at once; lighting up the architecture or building, and providing sharp contrast between the lighted object and its background. In silhouetting, a lighting fixture is placed behind a prominent object, such as a plant or statue and close enough to a wall to evenly light it. This will create a dark silhouette of the object on the backdrop of the wall.

Figure 13: Silhouetting a Tree or Large Plant

Shadowing

By placing a spotlight in front of a feature and aiming towards an adjacent wall, you create an illuminated backdrop with a dark shadow of the object projected on that wall. Using this technique, you can highlight and silhouette objects at the same time for a stunning result.

Figure 14: Shadowing

Wallwashing

Place a wide angle flood light up close to a wall or façade and shine the light upwards or sideways at a sharp angle so the beam is almost parallel to the face of the object. This will create an even glow across the wall or object it's pointed toward. This will also maintain an even and somewhat subtle ambient lighting for the nearby area. Indoors wall lights or sconces create a similar effect.

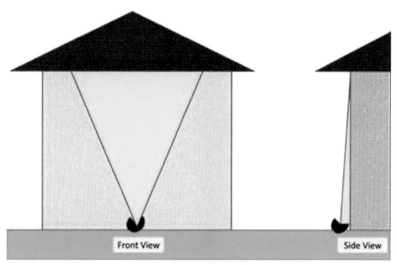

Figure 15: Wall washing from Front and Side

Down lighting

Involves mounting a flood light high up in a tree or a manmade structure with the light pointing downwards to light up a large area. The higher you place the light fixture, the larger the area of the yard that can be illuminated. For very high placements such as on top of the roof where the intent is to flood the entire yard with light, using strong, long-lasting lights bulbs such as Metal Halide are a good choice.

Figure 16: Down lighting

You can estimate how wide of an area will be lit up from different heights with the formula illustrated in Figure 17.

S = (2) x (D) x Tan(1/2 x A)

Where:

S = the spread of the beam at the surface being illuminated

D = the distance from the light source to the surface being illuminated

Tan = the tangent of the angle

A = the angle of the bean in the light bulb being used.

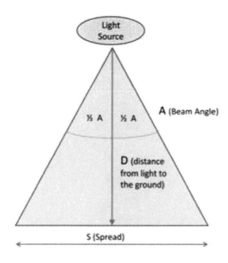

Figure 17: How to calculate the surface illuminated by a flood light

Some examples:

Light Type	Angle (degrees)	Tangent of 1/2 Angle
Narrow Spot Light	7 - 15	.11
Standard Spot Light	16 - 20	.16
Narrow Flood Light	21 - 30	.22
Standard Flood Light	31 - 40	.32
Wide Flood Light	41 - 60	.47

Table 1: Beam Angle and Tangent for Different Types of Bulbs

Using the numbers from the above table, a standard flood light 30 feet from the surface will illuminate an area approximately 20 feet across (2 x 30 x .32).

Another factor to consider is that the intensity of the light from a given bulb decreases by the square of the distance from the surface it is illuminating. So when down lighting, the higher you go, the wider the spread; but the light intensity as perceived at the surface becomes less. This is why metal halide lamps, with their powerful output are good choices for roof top fixtures that are used to light an entire yard.

Moonlighting

This technique places a flood lamp high up in a tree and angled down though the branches to create a dispersion of light and shadows across the scenery. As the name implies, this creates an effect that simulates moonlight shining down through the branches and projects dappled shadow patterns on the ground. The source of the illumination should be hidden from sight behind a branch or in the crotch of a tree so that a bright light is not clearly visible in the tree.

Figure 18: Moonlighting

Chapter 9

How to Make Your Backyard Water Features Shine at Night

Aquatic lights add night time ambiance to water gardens and increase the time that you can enjoy spending in your yard. Underwater lights transform dark and uninviting places by illuminating fish, plants, trees, rocks, fountains and waterfalls in a variety of magical ways.

Strategically positioning just a handful of these lights can add a whole new dimension to any water feature when the sun goes down. A shadow created by aquatic plants, ripples on the surface from waterfalls and fountains and even lights on the fish themselves create an atmosphere that cannot be experienced during the daylight hours.

Safety must always be the first consideration when adding aquatic lights to water gardens. Water and electricity don't mix and the consequences could be fatal. It is recommended to <u>only</u> use solar powered lights or low-voltage lights when working in and around water features. The cable and connections that come with underwater lights are waterproof but <u>do not pull on the wire</u> since it could damage a seal. Carefully follow the manufacturer's installation instructions. Obviously, all external connections should be above water and shielded from the environment.

Low-voltage Aquatic Lights

As already stated in this book, low-voltage electrical systems include a transformer to supply electricity. This power pack plugs into a standard outlet and reduces regular household current (120 volts) to a safe 12 volts. Most transformers have an automatic timer allowing lights to go on and off at preset times. Underwater low-voltage lamps connected by waterproof cable are available in a variety of colors, brightness levels and bulb types. Low-voltage, water-resistant, self-sealing, insulated copper wire is used to connect the lamps and transmit electricity. Low-voltage underwater lights are a tried-and-true solution that is easy to work with.

Solar Powered Aquatic Lights

The technology behind underwater solar lights has improved in recent years and batteries are more efficient and longer lasting in holding a charge. However they are still best suited for sunny climates and of course, work better in the summer with longer days and shorter nights. It is important to position the solar panel that powers the underwater light for maximum sun exposure.

For water features located where it is difficult or expensive to provide access to electricity, solar powered lights provide a viable alternative. LED (light emitting diodes) lights are particularly effective with solar power since they draw considerably less electricity than standard halogen bulbs and will stay lit for a much longer period of time on a given solar charge.

Locating Underwater Lights

Care must be taken when positioning underwater lights in a water garden. While just randomly placing the fixture on the bottom or sides of a pond or fountain may light up the water it will also expose debris or algae and may make the water appear cloudy. So don't place a light at the bottom of pond shining up and expect wonderful results. For spectacular effects, place underwater lights to illuminate specific water features such as rocks, plants or statues and especially moving water such as waterfalls, fountains and streams. Underwater lights come in different colors and when located behind waterfalls or under fountains create magnificent night time light shows. Underwater ring lights are especially effective in lighting fountains. Trial and error is the key in finding the best locations and angles for underwater lights so test different alternatives to see if you obtain the desired effect before permanently securing the fixture.

Lighting Ideas to Make Water Gardens Shine at Night

There are essentially 3 classes of lights that can be used to make a pond standout at night. They all can be found in either the halogen or LED form.

Submersible Pond Lights

As the name implies, submersible lights go underwater in the pond. Much like pool lights, submersible pond lights are intended to give the water a glowing ambiance and highlight fish and plants. However submersible pond lights will also illuminate "anything" that is in the water. So unless your pond water is exceptionally clear like a pool, submersible lights can make the water appear cloudier. For this reason, we prefer lighting the pond itself from above which makes the colorful koi standout at night against an opaque black background. Koi are very beautiful pond animals and seeing them illuminated at night brings out the shine of their scales and the beauty of their coloring. This contrast can be seen in Figure 19.

Where we find the use of submersible lights to be spectacular is in lighting waterfalls and fountains. Submersible pond lights come with different color lenses and can be located behind waterfalls or under fountains to create magnificent night time light shows. Submersible ring lights are especially effective with pond fountains (Figure 20).

Figure 19: Koi lit from above and ....from below

Figure 20: Fountain lit by ring light

Floating Pond Lights

For additional effects in the pond at night, you can add floating pond lights. Floating lights are fun to watch because they bob and move with the current in the pond. There are many different kinds available including special-effect lights that change colors gradually. They generally come as floating globes or in the shape of water lilies. Whatever style you choose, we recommend getting solar powered floating pond lights so there are no cords attached.

Figure 21: Floating Blue Light

General Landscape Lights

Landscape lights are the third type of lighting to make your pond and water features shine at night. This type of lighting can be used to frame the borders of the pond and to accent certain plants or features such as rocks or trees. If you don't light your pond waterfall from behind, spot lighting it from the front creates a nice shimmering effect. If you have any paths around your pond or your backyard in general, it's always a good idea to make sure the path is well lit for safe walking. Like floating and submersible lights, landscape lights are also available as solar lights so no wiring or electricity is needed.

Installing aquatic lighting is a natural extension of building or buying water features in the first place. A lighted water garden is beautiful and provides a way to enjoy your property at all hours. As with any other outdoor lighting, aquatic lights add to the security of the property. Effective landscaping also adds to the resale value. When installing aquatic lights, safety concerns must be paramount and where electrical work is required, unless you have the requisite knowledge, a professional should be called.

Chapter 10

LEDs, the Future of Lighting

In January 1879, at his laboratory in Menlo Park, New Jersey, Thomas Edison built his first high resistance, incandescent electric light bulb. It worked by passing electricity through a thin platinum filament in a glass vacuum bulb. The purpose of the vacuum was to extend the time before the filament melted. Even so, the lamp only burned for a few short hours. A little over 1 year later, Edison and his associates came up with a carbonized bamboo filament that lasted for 1,200 hours. Contrary to popular belief, Edison did not invent the electric light, which was first built by Englishman Humphry Davy eighty years earlier, but he did develop the first long-lasting, commercially viable light bulb.

Over 130 years later, Edison's "invention" is still the primary light source in the world. The carbon filaments have been replaced by tungsten, and incandescent light bulbs now have an average lifetime of 1500 to 2000 hours, but the basic design is essentially the same; electrical current running though and heating a filament, which gives off the light in a closed vacuum bulb.

Now for the first time, the continued market dominance of the incandescent light bulb is in serious question. This is not due to misguided government policies that attempt to force unpopular products on the public, but the presence of a viable challenger that is on the horizon.

LED, which stands for light emitting diodes, work on the principle of a solid state semi-conductor like a transistor. In simplest terms, illumination in a LED is a result of electrons moving within the semi-conducting structure of the light. There is no need for a vacuum or a filament which burns out nor is there the toxic mercury gas that exists in CFLs. Like transistors, LEDs do not get hot and last for a very long time. They also use far less electricity than the alternatives.

LEDs have been with us for years serving as the numbers in digital clocks, indicators on all sorts of appliances, transmitting signals from remote controls, and sometimes even Christmas lights. But until recently these tiny bulbs have never been used in mass to provide full room lighting. The key factors that determine the marketability of a light bulb are efficacy, color quality, life of the bulb, cost, and controllability. LEDs are approaching a tipping point on most of these criteria where it will soon be the preferred alternative over both incandescent bulbs and CFLs. LEDs already use less electricity and last much longer than either incandescent bulbs or CFLs. They can be built to emit different colors and are easily controllable by a dimmer. This all makes LED lights sound like a clear winner so what is holding them back?

LEDs have a very high upfront cost compared to other bulbs. Currently a 60 watt incandescent bulb sells in packages for about $1.25 per light. A 15 watt CFL bulb, which emits the same amount of light, cost around $6 while the equivalent LED is as high as $25. While this upfront cost is usually recouped by replacement and energy savings during the LED's very long (50,000 hours) life, many people are understandably hesitant about spending the initial money.

Table 4 compares costs for different bulbs over the LEDs 50,000 hour RTL.

	LED	CFL	Incandescent	Halogen
Projected Lifespan	50000	10000	1200	3000
Watts (equiv 60 watt bulb)	10	14	60	50
Cost Per Bulb	$25.00	$6.00	$1.25	$2.50
KWH used over 50K hours	500	700	3000	2500
Cost of electricity $0.12 per KWH	$60.00	$84.00	$360.00	$300.00
# of Bulbs over 50K hours	1	5	42	17
Cost of bulbs of 50K hours	$25.00	$30.00	$52.50	$42.50
Total Lifetime Cost	$85.00	$124.00	$412.50	$342.50

Table 1: Cost Comparison of Different Types of Lights

The good news is that the cost of LED's is coming down dramatically as the production process and materials improve and more manufacturers enter the market. Historically, the cost of LED's has come down by a factor of 10 every decade. If this trend continuous, in another 10 years or so, the $25 LED will cost only $2.50, which will be affordable for all lighting applications.

This will not require government interference in the marketplace since the public will buy LEDs simply because they are the best and most cost effective alternative available

About the Author

Bob Long was born in the Bronx, NY and grew up in a close-knit blue collar family. His education and work experience is in engineering, as a senior executive at Fortune 500 companies and a small business owner. He has worked in a variety of industries including transportation, finance, healthcare and technology. He has many interests including fishing, gardening, sports and surfing the Internet.

He likes to write about subjects where he has a passionate interest and can draw on his experience as an engineer, businessman and outdoors-man. He currently lives in Texas with his wife of 25+ years, 2 teen age children and bunch of dogs.

Other Books by Bob Long

Political Books

In His Own Words: 58 Reasons Not to Re-Elect President Barack Obama

DC Cuts: How the Federal Budget Defies Physics

EZ Guides

The EZ Guide To Building A Koi Pond

The EZ Guide To Dog Breeds

The EZ Guide to Aeroponics, Hydroponics, and Aquaponics

The EZ Guide to Hydroponics

The EZ Guide to Aquaponics

The EZ Guide to Aeroponics